DISNEY

ZOOTOPIA

Level 6

T0351214

Re-told by: Hawys Morgan
Series Editor: Rachel Wilson

Contents

In This Book

Judy Hopps

A rabbit who dreams of being Zootopia's best police officer

Nick Wilde

A smart fox who is full of surprises

Chief Bogo

Zootopia's top police officer

Mayor Lionheart

A lion who leads the animals of Zootopia

Deputy Mayor Bellwether

A sheep who works hard for Mayor Lionheart

Mr Otterton

A missing animal who Judy wants to find

Before You Read

Introduction

Judy Hopps was a small rabbit with big dreams. When she was little, Judy Hopps lived in the country with her family. She wanted to be a police officer, but her mom and dad were worried. Rabbits weren't police officers, they were farmers. That didn't stop Judy. She studied hard and got a job as a police officer in Zootopia. She believed it was a city where anyone could be anything. She believed it was a city where every animal was equal. Would the real Zootopia be the city of her dreams?

. . . .

Activities

1 **Which sentence is true, do you think?**

1 Zootopia is a modern and pleasant city.

2 Nick and Judy are both police officers.

3 Nick and Judy are old enemies.

2 **Which animals are predators? Which are prey? Use the *Glossary*.**

Judy   Nick   Mayor Lionheart   Chief Bogo   Deputy Mayor Bellwether

3 **Describe a good police officer.**

weak   brave   honest   naughty   strong   afraid

Welcome to Zootopia

Judy was the smallest animal at Zootopia Police Academy, but that didn't stop her. For months, she worked hard. Every day, she studied, she ran, and she climbed. She wanted to be the best police officer in Zootopia. By the end of her time at Zootopia Police Academy, Judy was the best student in her class! Assistant Mayor Bellwether gave Judy her badge and said, "It's a real proud day for us little guys."

Her family were happy, but they were worried, too. Her dad told her to be careful near foxes in the city.

It was Judy's first day in the capital city—Zootopia! She walked down the street and looked at the crowds of animals everywhere. There were big animals, small animals, loud animals, and quiet animals. Everyone lived together happily, every animal was equal.

It was very different than her home. Judy's family lived on a farm in the country. Her mom and dad were carrot farmers. Judy was the first rabbit in her family to live in the city, and the first police officer rabbit, too!

The next day, Judy started work at the ZPD—the Zootopia Police Department. The other police officers were much bigger than Judy, but she didn't mind. She listened carefully to Chief Bogo and took notes with her carrot pen.

Chief Bogo explained that fourteen animals were missing from the city. Chief Bogo was worried. Where were they? They might be lost or in trouble.

Judy was excited. She wanted to help. She said to Chief Bogo, "I was top of my class at the Police Academy." But Chief Bogo wanted Judy to write traffic tickets for cars. Judy was not pleased. She knew she was a good police officer.

Judy decided to work hard and show Chief Bogo that she was the bravest police officer in Zootopia.

Judy was writing a traffic ticket when she saw a fox in an ice-cream store for big animals. That was strange. Why was a fox in there?

She heard the fox say to the elephant, "I'm not looking for any trouble. I just want a Jumbo-pop for my little boy."

"Can't you go to a fox ice-cream store?" replied the elephant. The fox explained that his son loved elephants. And Jumbo-pops!

The fox's son was crying. Judy was angry. She explained that she was a police officer. She told the elephant to sell a Jumbo-pop to the fox. The elephant wasn't happy, but finally he agreed. The fox thanked Judy, but then he realized he didn't have any money. Judy felt bad so she bought the Popsicle for the fox.

Outside, the fox said, "Officer, I can't thank you enough, so kind." The fox said his name was Nick.

Judy told the little boy, "You be an elephant if you want. In Zootopia, anyone can be anything."

2 Criminals in the City

That afternoon, Judy was working in the city when she saw Nick and his son again. Judy watched them make the large Jumbo-pop into a lot of smaller Popsicles. And now he was selling them! This was wrong.

Also, the other fox wasn't his son. He wasn't even young—he could drive a car! Nick and his friend weren't honest. In fact, they were criminals!

Judy's mom and dad always said that she should be careful around foxes. Now Judy thought that they might be right!

Judy ran after Nick. She wanted answers. Nick understood that Judy had a dream of being a city police officer, but he didn't think it would happen. He thought she would go back to the country and become a carrot farmer.

"No one tells me what I can or can't be," shouted Judy.

Nick replied, "You can only be what you are." And in his opinion, rabbits were stupid. Judy shouted that she was not stupid. She tried to follow Nick, but she couldn't move her feet! "You'll never be a real police officer," said Nick.

The next day, a thief robbed flowers from a flower store. Judy followed the thief into Little Rodentia. Judy and the thief were much bigger than the mice who lived there. Cars had to stop suddenly. Mice ran left and right, escaping Judy's big feet.

Finally, Judy caught the thief and she took him to Chief Bogo, "Sir, I got the bad guy. That's my job."

Judy thought that Chief Bogo would be happy with her. He was not. He was angry about the trouble in Little Rodentia, "Your job is putting tickets on parked cars!"

3 | Where Is Mr. Otterton?

Suddenly, the door opened. "Chief Bogo, please," said a sad voice. "My husband has been missing for ten days. His name is Emmitt Otterton. He has a flower store and two beautiful children. He would never just disappear."

Judy jumped up, "I will find him!"

Mrs. Otterton was grateful and gave Judy a photo of Mr. Otterton, "Take this. Find my Emmitt."

Then Deputy Mayor Bellwether arrived. She was happy that Judy was helping Mrs. Otterton. Chief Bogo was unhappy, "I will give you 48 hours. That's two days to find Emmitt Otterton." If Judy failed, she would leave the police.

Judy didn't have much information about Mr. Otterton. She looked closely at the only photo of him. She noticed that in the photo he was eating one of Nick's Popsicles!

Judy found Nick. At first, Nick didn't want to help, but finally he agreed. Together, they discovered that a big, white car took Mr. Otterton.

It was night when they found the car. When they opened the door, they saw that inside it was messy and there was fur everywhere! Judy found a photo of Mr. Otterton in the car. "What do you think happened?" asked Judy.

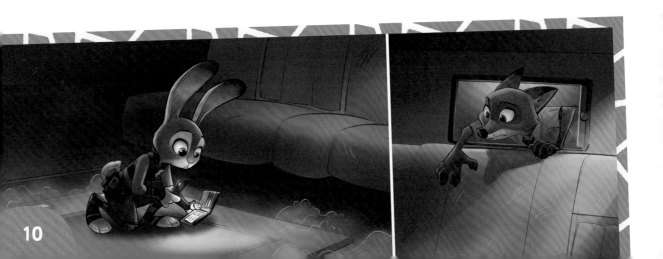

It didn't look good for Mr. Otterton. Judy needed more information.

Nick and Judy found the driver of the car, Mr. Manchas. He slowly opened the door a little. Judy saw he was hurt and scared. She said, "We just want to know what happened to Emmitt Otterton."

He replied, "You should be asking what happened to me!"

Then Mr. Manchas described what happened the night Mr. Otterton disappeared. Mr. Otterton was sitting quietly in the car. Suddenly, he became wild. He walked on four legs. He shouted about the night howlers again and again. Night howlers? What were *night howlers*?

Judy wanted to know more. They waited for Mr. Manchas to open the door. But then they heard strange noises coming from inside the house. Judy carefully pushed open the door. "Are you okay?" she asked.

The driver turned his head and looked at them with fierce eyes. He was wild, like Mr. Otterton! "Run! *RUN!*" shouted Judy as Mr. Manchas jumped at them.

He followed them outside, running on four legs. Judy and Nick were frightened. At last, Judy locked Mr. Manchas to a street light, but then Judy and Nick fell through the jungle trees below.

4 Night Howlers

Chief Bogo arrived. Judy explained that Mr. Otterton didn't just disappear—he was wild! But he didn't believe her.

She took Chief Bogo to the street light, but Mr. Manchas wasn't there! Chief Bogo was angry with Judy, "Badge!" he shouted, holding out his hand.

But then Nick stopped him. "No!"

"What did you say, Fox?" replied Chief Bogo.

Nick explained, "You gave Officer Hopps 48 hours to find Mr. Otterton and we still have 10 hours left!" Then he and Judy left together.

Judy was surprised that Nick was helping her. Maybe foxes weren't so bad after all? "Thank you," she said quietly.

Nick explained that other animals were mean to him because he was a fox. Chief Bogo was mean to Judy because she was a rabbit. He understood how Judy felt.

As they talked, Nick looked down at the traffic below them. Suddenly, he had a great idea. They could look at the city's traffic cameras to find the driver. Perhaps Deputy Mayor Bellwether would help them?

They arrived at Zootopia Town Hall and heard Mayor Lionheart shouting at Deputy Mayor Bellwether, "I'm going out." He was very rude to her.

Deputy Mayor Bellwether was happy to help them. Together, they looked at the traffic cameras. A group of wolves found Mr. Manchas locked to the street light. They took him and put him in a truck. Then one of the wolves howled.

"That's it!" thought Judy. "Wolves howl at night so *night howlers* must mean wolves!" If the wolves took Mr. Manchas, maybe they took Mr. Otterton, too?

They followed the truck on the cameras. It drove out of the city and stopped at Cliffside Asylum.

Nick and Judy raced there. A group of wolves were guarding the gates, but Judy had a great idea. She hid behind the gates and howled! Soon, all the wolf-guards were howling, too. The guards were so busy howling, they didn't see Judy and Nick pass through the gate and enter Cliffside Asylum. Nick smiled at Judy. She was a smart rabbit.

Inside Cliffside Asylum

Cliffside Asylum was dark, but Nick and Judy were brave and they went inside. They found what they wanted: Mr. Otterton and Mr. Manchas! In the past, Cliffside Asylum was a hospital, but now it was a prison.

They found poor Mr. Otterton in a cage. There were other animals in cages. Judy counted them, "… eleven, twelve, thirteen, fourteen." All the missing animals were there, and they were all wild!

What happened to these animals? Why were they wild? Suddenly, the door opened so Judy and Nick jumped into an empty cage and hid.

Mayor Lionheart came into the room with a doctor. Judy recorded the conversation on her phone. The mayor shouted at the doctor, "Enough! I don't want excuses, Doctor. I need answers!"

"Mayor Lionheart, please," replied the doctor. "We're doing everything we can."

Mayor Lionheart pointed to the wild animals in their cages. He didn't think the doctor was doing enough. The doctor explained that all the wild animals were predators, "We cannot keep it a secret!"

Mayor Lionheart didn't agree. He thought it should stay a secret because he was a predator, too. Then Judy's parents called her …

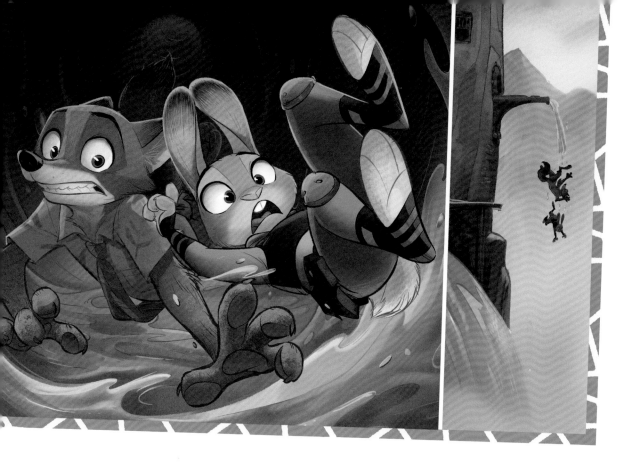

Mayor Lionheart heard the cell phone. "Someone's here!" he shouted.

The wolf-guards were arriving. Nick and Judy needed to escape, but they were in a cage, with no way out! Judy looked around the cage then asked Nick, "Can you swim?"

"What! Can I swim? Yes, I can swim. Why?" asked Nick. Judy pointed to the large toilet. They fell down, down, down the toilet until … *SPLASH!*

They hit the lake. At first, Nick couldn't find Judy in the water. He was worried and shouted out her name. Then, he found her, and she still had her phone!

Judy told Chief Bogo about Cliffside Asylum. The police arrived at the secret prison where they found Mayor Lionheart, the doctor and the missing animals.

As Judy took Mayor Lionheart away, he said to her, "You don't understand. I was trying to protect the city."

But Judy didn't believe him and she replied angrily, "You were trying to protect your job!"

"Listen," he said. "We still don't know why this is happening." He thought it could be the end of Zootopia.

6 A New Mayor

Everybody wanted to know about the wild animals found at Cliffside Asylum. First, Chief Bogo said thank you to Judy. Then, Judy answered the crowd's questions. They wanted to know why it was happening.

Judy explained that all the wild animals were predators. They didn't know exactly why it was happening, but maybe it was because they were predators. Many years ago, predators attacked weaker prey animals, and now it was happening again. It was important for everybody to be careful.

Judy stopped answering questions and returned to Nick. "That went so fast!" she said.

Nick replied, "Oh, I think you said … plenty". He couldn't believe what Judy said to the crowd. Foxes were predators, too. Did Judy think *he* was dangerous?

Judy said, "You're not like them!"

"Oh, there's a 'them' now?" said Nick.

"You know what I mean. You're not that kind of predator," replied Judy.

"Let me ask you a question. Are you scared of me?" asked Nick. "Do you think I might try to eat you?" Nick walked away. He felt sad and angry.

Everyone in Zootopia was scared. Prey animals were afraid of predators. Neighbors fought each other. Life in the city became terrible.

The new mayor, Mayor Bellwether, wanted to meet with Judy and Chief Bogo. She thought Judy could help prey animals in Zootopia feel less nervous. Judy replied sadly, "I came here to make the world a better place, but I think I broke it."

"The world has always been broken, that's why we need good officers, like you," said Chief Bogo. But Judy gave back her badge. She didn't think she was a good officer.

Judy decided to leave Zootopia and go home to the country. She felt unhappy, but she tried to hide it from her parents. She was selling vegetables when suddenly her dad shouted at some young rabbits. "Hey, children! Don't run through the blue flowers!"

Then a neighbor said, "My family always called them night howlers."

Judy's dad explained that he grew the flowers because they kept insects away from his vegetables. Then he told Judy a story about one of her uncles. Years ago, her uncle ate one of the flowers and became wild ...

7 Return to Zootopia

Night howlers? The flowers were called *night howlers*! Judy immediately jumped in the farm truck and drove back to the city.

She found Nick, "Night howlers aren't wolves!" She told him that night howlers were flowers that made animals become wild. Someone was using the flowers on predators. But Nick didn't want to talk. He walked away.

"Wait!" Judy called out. "I know you'll never forgive me." Judy wanted to help the predators in Zootopia, but she couldn't do it without Nick.

Nick turned and smiled at her, "Don't worry." They were friends again.

Nick ate blueberries in the truck as Judy drove. Judy described the thief who stole blue flowers in Little Rodentia. The flowers might be night howlers!

With Nick's help, they found the thief. The thief said he stole the flowers for a ram called Doug.

The thief's information took them to a railroad under the city. They climbed inside a train and watched Doug the ram. He used night howler flowers to produce a blue serum. They listened to Doug talk on the phone. He described shooting Mr. Otterton with the night howler serum. Judy had to tell the police!

Judy wanted to show the night howlers to the police. She decided to take the whole train to the police.

When Doug wasn't looking, Judy pushed him out of the train. She ran to the front of the train and started to drive it. But some other rams ran after them. They jumped on the train, climbed on the roof, and jumped through a hole.

The train moved faster and faster through the city into a station. The train was moving too fast—it was dangerous!

Judy Finds the Criminal

Nick and Judy jumped off the train. They reached the station platform just before the train hit a wall. *CRASH!*

Fire burned all the night howler flowers inside the train. Without the flowers, how could Judy tell the police what was happening? Nick smiled at her and pulled out a case from behind his back. It was Doug's case! The dart and night howler serum were inside it.

Judy laughed, "Nick, yes! Come on, we've got to get to the ZPD."

Judy remembered there was a quicker way to the police station through the museum. She and Nick ran up some steps into the museum and raced toward the doors. Judy was surprised to hear someone calling her name. It was Mayor Bellwether and two guards.

"We found out what's happening," said Judy. Mayor Bellwether listened as Judy explained. Someone was shooting predators with a serum. It made them go wild.

"I'm so proud of you, Judy," replied Mayor Bellwether, as she reached for the case.

Something wasn't right. "How did you know where to find us?" Judy asked Mayor Bellwether.

Mayor Bellwether tried to take the case, but Judy said, "Nick and I will just take this to the ZPD." But when she and Nick turned around, they saw a big guard at the museum entrance. He didn't look very friendly.

Nick and Judy both said, "Run!" and they escaped into the museum.

"Get them!" called Mayor Bellwether. She and the guards followed Judy and Nick through the museum.

A guard knocked the case out of Nick's hand. Judy and Nick fell
to the floor. Mayor Bellwether picked up the case and laughed,
"It really is too bad. I did like you."

Judy looked up at Mayor Bellwether and asked, "What are you
going to do? Kill me?"

Mayor Bellwether replied, "No, of course not. He is!"

Then she shot Nick with the dart! It hit him in the neck and he
dropped to the floor. Judy ran to his side. Was he okay? She held
him and said, "No, Nick, don't do this. Fight it!"

Mayor Bellwether phoned the police and told them there was a wild fox in the museum, "Officer Hopps is down. Please hurry!"

Mayor Bellwether explained her plan. She wanted prey animals to be scared of predators.

"So that's it—prey animals are afraid of predator animals—and you stay in power?" asked Judy.

"That's the plan!" replied Bellwether. "I'll shoot every predator in Zootopia to keep it that way."

"It won't work!" cried Judy.

Suddenly, Nick jumped at Judy. He was wild! She ran away from him, but he ran after her. Mayor Bellwether looked down at them and smiled.

Nick got closer and closer to Judy. He opened his mouth to bite her. His teeth were on her neck. Judy screamed loudly.

Mayor Bellwether couldn't believe it when Judy stood up and started talking. Nick wasn't wild and Judy was okay. What was happening?

Nick said to Mayor Bellwether, "Are you looking for the serum? Well, it's right here."

Judy pointed at Mayor Bellwether's hand. "What you've got there—those are blueberries from my family's farm," she explained.

Nick laughed, "They are delicious! You should try some." Mayor Bellwether checked. Judy was right!

Mayor Bellwether was angry now, "It's my word against yours!"

Judy smiled at Mayor Bellwether and then pulled out her carrot pen. The carrot pen could record what people said. Judy played it and they all heard Mayor Bellwether say, "I'll shoot every predator in Zootopia to keep it that way …"

"It's your word against yours!" Judy was enjoying this.

Now Mayor Bellwether was really worried. She tried to escape, but when she turned around, she saw Chief Bogo with a team of police officers. They took Mayor Bellwether to prison.

9 A New Police Officer

Mayor Bellwether went to prison. And Lionheart came out of prison. He understood now that it was a mistake to lock up the wild predators.

Slowly, things got better in the city. Prey and predators became friends again. There was more good news for Zootopia. Doctors found a medicine to help all the wild predators.

Mr. Otterton woke up in the hospital. He wasn't wild now—he was nice Mr. Otterton again. Mrs. Otterton was very grateful to Judy, "Thank you!" she said.

Then, an important day arrived. Judy stood in front of the other police officers and said:

"When I was a young rabbit, I thought Zootopia was a perfect place. I thought everyone lived happily together. But real life is messy. We all make mistakes, but we have to try to understand each other. It doesn't matter what animal you are, from the biggest elephant to our first fox. Please try. Try to make the world a better place."

Then she gave Nick his badge. He was a police officer now—the first fox police officer in Zootopia!

After You Read

1 **Put the sentences into the correct order.**

a Mayor Bellwether goes to prison.

b Judy catches a thief stealing blue flowers.

c Mr. Manchas becomes wild.

d Nick makes small Popsicles.

e Judy and Nick find the wild animals.

f Judy becomes a police officer.

g Judy discovers that the blue flowers make animals wild.

2 **Describe how Nick changes from the start of the story to the end.**

3 **What job would you like to do in Zootopia? Why?**

mayor   doctor   police officer   driver   actor
scientist   teacher   engineer   chef   musician

4 **Why might prey animals feel afraid of predator animals? Discuss with a friend.**

Glossary

badge (*noun*) a piece of metal or plastic that you wear to show where you work

blueberry (*noun*) a small, round, dark blue fruit

cage (*noun*) a box made of metal for keeping animals and birds

carrot (*noun*) a long, orange vegetable that grows under the ground

dart (*noun*) something sharp that flies through the air

equal (*adj.*) the same

farmer (*noun*) someone who works on a farm

fierce (*adj.*) a fierce person or animal is angry or ready to attack, and looks very frightening

fox (*noun*) an animal that looks like a small dog with dark red fur

howl past tense **howled** (*verb*) to make a long, loud sound. Wolves and dogs howl; *Wolves howl at night so night howlers must mean wolves!*

like (*prep.*) in the same way

Popsicle (*noun*) a food; ice on a stick, made of fruit juice

predator (*noun*) an animal that kills and eats other animals

prey (*noun*) an animal that other animals eat

protect past tense **protected** (*verb*) to keep someone or something away from danger; *"You don't understand. I was trying to protect the city."*

ram (*noun*) a male sheep

record past tense **recorded** (*verb*) to save pictures, sound, or music so that you can watch or listen to it again; *The carrot pen could record what people said.*

serum (*noun*) something that looks like water; you put serum on, or into, your body

wild (*adj.*) acting in a dangerous, frightening way; *Someone was shooting predators with a serum. It made them go wild.*

wolf (*noun*) an animal that looks like a large gray dog

Play: Stand Up to Bullies

Scene 1:

A young fox is bullying some little sheep and rabbits. Young Judy sees this.

FOX: Give me your tickets, you weak little sheep!

SHEEP: [very afraid, handing over the tickets]: O-o-kay. Here you go.

FOX: [takes the tickets] What are you going to do? Cry? [laughs]: Ha ha ha!

JUDY: Please return those tickets to my friends!

FOX: Huh? Come and get them, but be careful because I'm a fox. We predators used to eat prey!

JUDY: I'm not afraid of you!

Scene 2:

The fight begins. The fox is bigger than Judy but she's brave.

JUDY: You're just a big bully!

FOX: And you're a stupid rabbit!

He pushes Judy to the ground, but she gets the tickets out of his pocket. Then he walks away.

Scene 3:

After the fight.

JUDY: [giving the tickets back to the sheep] Here are your tickets.

SHEEP: Thank you. You're so brave, Judy!

RABBIT: You showed him!

JUDY: [walking away] I'm *not* a stupid rabbit.

Global Citizenship

Bullying, No Way!

Just like Judy Hopps, Jaylen Arnold has been brave since he was a child. At school, children bullied Jaylen because he was different. The bullies said horrible things to him and pushed him around. He cried at night because he felt so bad. One day, Jaylen decided to do something about it. He started a charity to teach children around the world how to fight bullying.

Bullying doesn't just happen at school. It can happen on the Internet or in phone messages, too. Jaylen's charity teaches children that we are all equal, even when we are different. Jaylen travels around schools, goes on television, and writes in magazines. He shares his important message: Bullying, No Way!

Find Out

What is a food chain?

A food chain shows how plants and animals get their food. It also shows how plants and animals need one another to survive.

A food chain starts with a producer. A producer is a living thing that makes its own food. In most food chains, the producer is a plant. Plants use sunlight to make their own food. Next in the food chain is a consumer. A consumer is a living thing that eats other plants and animals.

sunlight

grass (producer)

mouse (consumer)

bird (consumer)

This grass is at the start of the food chain. It can make its own food. It is a producer.

This mouse eats the grass. It can't make its own food. It is a consumer.

This bird eats the mouse. It is at the top of the food chain. It is a consumer.

Predators and Prey

In *Zootopia*, predators and prey live happily together. In real life, a predator is an animal that eats other animals. The animals that predators eat are called prey. Predators are at the top of a food chain.

Rabbits and Foxes

Rabbits are consumers. They only eat grass and other plants. They are prey.

Foxes are consumers, too, but they eat lots of different foods. Sometimes they are predators. They catch and eat mice, frogs, and rabbits. They also eat a lot of plants and fruit.

survive (*verb*) to continue to live

Phonics

Say the sounds. Read the words.

le

(jungle)   (purple)

al

(capital)   (criminal)

Read, then say the rhyme to a friend.

Nick was a criminal,
But he wasn't horrible.
Judy liked vegetables.
She was very sensible.

They looked for an animal,
Missing in the capital.
They found him in the hospital.
Anything is possible!